RED ALERT! IS HE THE ONE? WORKBOOK:
POCKET GUIDE TO FINDING
THE LOVE OF YOUR LIFE

TANYA E. HOOD

WITH: TIFFANY D. ALEXANDER

TESTIMONY PUBLISHERS, LLC.

Jackson, Wyoming

THANK YOU FOR YOUR PURCHASE

As a small gesture of my appreciation, I'd like to offer you access to a free chapter in my premier book:

Chapter 1:
Red Alert! Is He The One? Pocket Guide To Finding The Love Of Your Life

http://bit.ly/RedAlertChapter1

If you have any questions or comments, please contact me at:

TanyaEHood@Outlook.com

I look forward to reading your comments, answering your questions, and celebrating your wins as you move closer to finding the love of your life!

GET YOUR POCKET GUIDE!

RED ALERT! IS HE THE ONE? WORKBOOK:
The Pocket Guide To Finding The Love Of Your Life
By: Tanya E. Hood
With: Tiffany D. Alexander

PUBLISHED BY:
Testimony Publishers, LLC.,
P.O. Box 2869
Jackson, Wyoming 83001
https://testimonypublishers.com/apply

COVER DESIGN:
Anointed Press Graphics, Inc., Copyright © 2017
Testimony Publishers, LLC, Copyright © 2019

Printed in the United States of America
ISBN: 978-1-7331394-0-3

The Author is available for book signings, public readings, conferences, events, (church, government agency, non-profit, professional association, & medical association), and business networking opportunities. Send your requests to TanyaEHood@outlook.com with the subject line *BOOKINGS*.

If you are a book club, association, organization, or special interest group and you want to inquire about bulk orders, contact the Author at TanyaEHood@outlook.com or Testimony Publishers, LLC. at admin@testimonypublishersllc.online with the subject line *BULK ORDER*.

CONTENTS

I want to take the time to thank you for choosing to do the work to get yourself to a better position. I commend you for choosing to love yourself and try for yourself. As women, we were designed to love, so we go searching to find the love we feel we need. Usually, we end up with *the user*, *the idiot*, or *the smooth talker* that does absolutely nothing to further our growth and development.

While the title of the book gives the impression that much of the pocket guide and workbook will seem like you are focusing on finding *Mr. Right*, you'll learn that you will have gained insight on who the "Perfect You" truly is. This will be defined in so many ways from reader to reader as each of you dive into matters of the spirit.

We will walk through the seven chapters of the pocket guide.

Chapter 1 – Get Clearance
Chapter 2 – Use Your Time Wisely
Chapter 3 – The Man Finds the Wife
Chapter 4 – Patterns
Chapter 5 – Intentions
Chapter 6 – Complimentary
Chapter 7 – The Example

Each chapter in this workbook is loaded with valuable lessons and insights. Just like the pocket guide, this workbook is structured to complete powerful lessons in a timeframe that is manageable. I know what it is like trying to grow personally, emotionally, spiritually, and otherwise. My goal is to leave you inspired and ready to learn what it will take for you to get to your next level. I've always enjoyed helping and encouraging people to do their best. I encourage you to challenge the situations in your life that make you feel less than you were designed to be (Psalm 139:14).

Now, let's get started on this journey!

CHAPTER 1: GET CLEARANCE

- ✓ I **NEVER** knew my father.
- ✓ **STRONG** women led my home.
- ✓ I got **MARRIED** at 21, with a **NEW BABY.**

Check Point!

DESCRIBE YOUR IDEAL MATE	DESCRIBE THE MATE YOU USUALLY END UP CHOOSING

If your list looks like I am guessing, the two sides probably don't add up! ☺ Don't worry, sit back, reflect, relax, and get ready to re-evaluate the way you once looked at it all. Pretty soon, you'll look at this list again, and it will make you smile. You may even decide to burn it in a fire pit or grill (my personal favorite), or discard it in a shredder! Let's keep moving.

Moment to *Inspire*...

To acquire wisdom is to love oneself; people who cherish understanding will prosper.

~Proverbs 19:8

How do we weed through the mess, so we don't get stuck with the guy that fronts with his boys about all he does for us and then sits on the couch at home waiting for us to do everything for him, like he's some king? Some say, *Look for the finest man you see.* Some say, *Choose a provider.* Some say, *Choose a man like your father.* Oftentimes, do you know what type of man we usually end up with at the end of the day? We usually choose a man that basically mirrors all of the men we were surrounded by while growing up. Sometimes we choose just the opposite of what we knew growing up. But trust and believe, if the men you model your mate after are not true men of God, you will ultimately end up with the very qualities you hate.

1. What are your expectations of a mate?

2. How do you "vet" a mate to determine if you've made the right decision?

3. The decisions you make regarding the man of your dreams must be made on a spiritual and intellectual basis before it is made on an emotional one. Do you know who you are outside of anything physical?

4. How do you define love?

5. Where did you learn the definition of love?

Moment to *R*eflect...

In Genesis 2:22, God brought Eve to Adam. Eve did not go man hunting. She did not even know that Adam existed. Eve was birthed in God's presence and HE was all she knew. WE MUST ALSO TAKE THE TIME TO BE BIRTHED IN GOD'S PRESENCE.

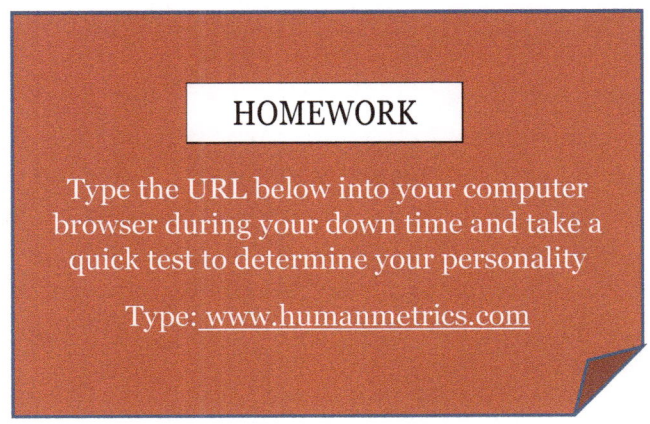

HOMEWORK

Type the URL below into your computer browser during your down time and take a quick test to determine your personality

Type: www.humanmetrics.com

You've heard the saying, "The heart wants, what the heart wants." How many times did you end up in a relationship that was disastrous because your heart led the way? "He's cute and he's paying attention to me. He must be the one." "He's called every day this week, he must be the one." Somewhere along the way our hearts defined love for us.

When considering love, look at God's definition (1 Corinthians 13:4-7, NLT):

> *4Love is patient and kind. Love is not jealous or boastful or proud 5or rude. It does not demand its own way. It is not irritable, and it keeps no record of being wronged. 6It does not rejoice about injustice but rejoices whenever the truth wins out. 7Love never gives up, never loses faith, is always hopeful, and endures through every circumstance.*

Who knew one little word had such a deep meaning? God sent me on a 3-year journey to truly discover *His* definition of love. Those 3 years were such an eye-opener. I discovered how orderly God is in everything. I could not show kindness until I learned patience. If I was kind, there was less likelihood of being rude. God wrote the definition of love to help you achieve it. Every word is a stepping-stone to help you achieve the next phase.

*Guard your heart above all else, for
it determines the course of your life.*

~ Proverbs 4:23

Check out his attributes, and then allow your heart to engage.

1. Does he make you feel like an amazing woman?

2. Does he treat you with the care and respect you deserve?

3. What little thing does he do that makes your heart melt?

RED ALERT:

This is the time to collect data. You need to know all you can, so you can be wise in the relationship. I believe that the biblical design of a meaningful relationship would be friendship, courtship, and *then* marriage.

CHAPTER 2: USE YOUR TIME WISELY

- ✓ I **LEARNED** about dating at 14.
- ✓ I **THOUGHT** a contract would keep a relationship together.
- ✓ **GATHER** the facts you need to have a **SUCCESSFUL** relationship.

Check Point!

DESCRIBE YOUR PLAN FOR TRAVELING	DESCRIBE YOUR PLAN FOR DATING

If you are anything like I was, you have a better travel plan than you do a dating plan. My grandmother told me that a job gives you 90 days to see if they want you working for them. During those 90 days, they look at your performance, your attitude, and determine if the way you conduct yourself will be good for their business. I don't believe we should expect anything less.

Moment to *Inspire*...

May He give you the desire of your heart and make all your plans succeed.

~Psalm 20:4

A job investigates your past to see if your word matches what is gathered about you. Essentially, does your character match your reputation? The referrals you provide will reveal your reputation. Your reputation is the opinion someone has about you. Your character shows your behavior and attitude, the real you. They observe you during the probation period.

1. What is your probationary period to evaluate a relationship?

2. What characteristics do you look for to determine if you've made the right decision?

3. Do you take the time to assess the reputation and character of your mate?

Moment to **R**eflect...

1 Timothy 3:1-10, basically says he must first want to have that role. Too often, we are looking for a husband in a man that does not want to be a husband. MOST MEN DECIDE TO GET MARRIED AND THEN LOOK FOR A WIFE.

HOMEWORK

Type the URL below into your computer browser during your down time and take a look at the character traits to determine the ones you think fit best into your life.

Type: **http://bit.ly/RedAlertCharacter**

Too often, we decide the man we are with is marriage material because we have been dating him for a while or, in my case, he was basically a good guy and we were already going to have a baby together. I failed to ask my ex-husband if he really wanted to marry me or if I fit the image he created in his mind of what a wife would be. So, I came up with the following questions during my observation in the aftermath of my divorce.

1. Is he marriage material?

2. Does he want a wife?

3. Does he want you?

4. Is he respected and held accountable?

5. Is he a lover of money?

6. Is he a part of the family of God?

A man grounded in God knows he will be tested to develop the type of behavior that pleases God. I have already shared that 90 days is a good test period. During this time of testing, abstain from sex. Yes, no nookie, no cookie, no whoopee, no coitus!

Whatever you have titled that moment, don't do it!

Sex clouds people's judgment. Besides, a respectable man of God will not allow you to compromise yourself. He will not engage in sex before marriage. Testing doesn't mean that this man has performed flawlessly on each and every character trait listed, but that he has allowed time for examination and to determine if he has gained the approval of God for his commitment to spiritual growth.

There is nothing wrong with a man that works hard, but he should not be a lover of money. A man driven by money will one day look at you as one of his trinkets instead of the Queen God designed you to be. If he sees you through God's eyes, he will manage his own household well and keep his children obedient because he will be following God's guidelines.

Examples of positive character traits:

• Religious	• Loving	• Ambitious
• Honest	• Kind	• Faithful
• Loyal	• Sincere	• Patient
• Devoted	• Happy	• Satisfied

Examples of character traits that can be developed, learned or acquired:

• Dauntless	• Brave	• Loving
• Strong	• Charming	• Affectionate
• Courageous	• Daring	• Charismatic
• Reliable	• Tough	• Fearless

CHAPTER 3: THE MAN FINDS THE WIFE

- ✓ I **DECIDED** I was done with marriage.
- ✓ I **ENCOUNTERED** the representatives.
- ✓ I **WALKED** through the 4 basic **STAGES** of a relationship.

Check Point!

DESCRIBE YOUR LIST OF MUST-HAVES FOR YOUR MATE	COMPARE YOUR LIST TO 1 TIMOTHY 3:1-10 AND ISAIAH 32:1-8
	Faithful
	Self-controlled
	Respectable
	Hospitable
	Honest
	Sincere
	Protector
	Respected
	Comforting
	Plans
	Not given to drunkenness
	Not violent but gentle
	Not quarrelsome
	Not conceited
	Not a lover of money
	Communicates well
	People watch for his guidance
	People listen to him
	Knows he will be tested

I came up with a list of 20 things that were my must-haves. I had to learn that a list was not going to cover everything I truly wanted or needed in my mate. I learned through this that I had to trust God's word.

Moment to *Inspire*...

Trust in the Lord with all your heart; do not depend on your own understanding. Seek His will in all you do, and He will show you which path to take.

~Proverbs 3:5-6

We are complex and constantly changing. Our relationships evolve and change as well. In my journey to getting a better understanding about what was happening in my life I discovered 4 basic stages to a relationship.

1. Pseudo-Relationship – This is typically a surface relationship where pleasantries are exchanged, but no one reveals who they truly are. This is the home of the representative. If you don't pay attention during this stage, you could be stuck here 6 months to a year.

2. Emergent-Relationship – This is where chaos reigns. You get to know each other better, but not too deep. You begin to notice some differences in what you initially believed about this person, but you typically dismiss it because the attraction is growing and the need to impress suppresses you from seeing the mess.

3. Becoming-Relationship – This is typically where you begin to empty yourself completely into this relationship. Hormones have calmed down enough for you to start letting go of some pretenses and more flaws (and weaknesses) are noticed. Arguments typically happen frequently in this stage. You begin to wonder where this relationship is headed. If you can

communicate your concerns, you will make it to the final stage.

4. <u>Committed-Relationship</u> - At this stage, you should know the flaws of the relationship and have decided to still press on in love anyway. You are authentic in who you are and fight to sustain the relationship despite what others say, think, or do.

*Moment to **R**eflect...*

Just like Eve knew Adam was her man, you will know the one God has chosen for you as well. Your responsibility is to be about the task God has called you to do. Besides, I heard it said that the man you really want is the one God has to tap on the shoulder to say, "LOOK UP, SHE'S THE ONE FOR YOU."

HOMEWORK

Type the URL below into your computer browser during your down time and take the focus on marriage assessment. I found this site to be very helpful in numerous ways.

Type: www.focusonthefamily.com

Personal development is the key to unlocking your breakthrough.

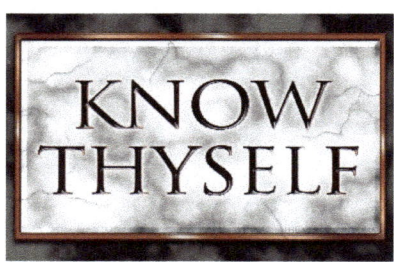

When you decide to become a better version of yourself it will be difficult. Be patient with yourself. It's OK if it takes you longer than you anticipated, because it will.

Take a moment to understand the motives and values that drive your behavior.

1. Do you have a strong desire to help people?

2. Do you have a strong desire to achieve results?

3. Do you have a strong desire to develop logical solutions?

The Strength Deployment Inventory (SDI) test can help you gain some insight into how your motivation reflects your values.

You may also want to take a look at the Myers–Briggs Type Indicator (MBTI). It, basically, says that what people know determines what they will do.

1. Are you bold, imaginative and strong-willed?

2. Do you find it easy to connect with others?

3. Do you prefer to analyze your surroundings and check the facts before arriving at practical courses of action.

I praise you because you made me in such a wonderful way.
I know how amazing that was.
~Psalm 139:14

Proverbs 31:10-31 gives a great synopsis of a woman that truly knew herself. I applied one or two things over time from this scripture and it has helped me discover myself and become the woman I desired to be.

Evaluate yourself.

- ✓ Check off the qualities you possess and <u>Underline</u> those you would like to start implementing:
- ☐ Trustworthy (v.11)
- ☐ Prosperous (v.12)
- ☐ A Fashion Designer (v.13)
- ☐ An Importer (v.14.)
- ☐ A Project Manager (v.15)
- ☐ A Realtor (v.16)
- ☐ An Energetic, Strong, and Hard Worker (v. 17)
- ☐ A Financial Analyst (v.18)
- ☐ A Textile Manager (v.19)
- ☐ Charitable (v.20)
- ☐ Home Economist (v.21, v.27)
- ☐ Seamstress (v.22)
- ☐ Lucrative Business Owner (v.24)
- ☐ Strong and Dignified (v.25)
- ☐ Well-Spoken (v.26)
- ☐ A God-Fearing Woman (v. 30)

1. Are you satisfied with what you discovered?

2. What are you willing to do to get better?

While studying the Proverbs 31 woman, I discovered there is never any mention about her appearance. Her attractiveness came entirely from her character. It was her outstanding abilities that caused her to be "more precious than rubies" (v. 10). Her amazing achievements came from her reverence for God.

CHAPTER 4: PATTERNS

- ✓ Birds of a feather **FLOCK** together.
- ✓ Never **FORGET** God made **YOU** wonderful and glorious.
- ✓ Don't stay **FOCUSED** on the foot, check out the rest of the body.

Check Point!

LIST SOME BAD HABITS	LIST YOUR BAD HABITS

It's often easy for us to come up with a list bad habits that deal with time, health, or productivity, like being late, smoking, and procrastination. It's very hard to identify the bad habits of relationships. If we never take the time to discover our bad relationship habits, we will continually carry them into new relationships.

Moment to *Inspire*...

Don't be conformed to the patterns of this world, but be transformed by the renewing of your mind so that you can figure out what God's will is—what is good and pleasing and mature.

~Romans 12:2

I had a habit of overlooking the flaws and issues I knew about the people I was in relationship with. I'm not just talking about dating. I did this with relatives and friends as well. I was under the impression that if I overlooked their flaws and issues, while exposing them to information and new circumstances, things would get better.

The problem is that bad habits die hard. Don't be blinded by what you want to believe versus what you actually know and can see. Everyone knows how to put their best foot forward. Don't stay focused on the foot, check out the rest of the body!

1. Do you find yourself repeating cycles of bad habits? If so, what do you think can help you break the bad habits?

2. What does your past reveal about the habits you've brought into current relationships?

3. The friends people choose reveals a lot to you about the person that you haven't seen yet. Have you taken the time evaluate their friends? What do you know?

4. Remember that a person's family reveals the cloth from which they are cut. Evaluate and decide whether you want your future with the man in your life to look like his present family situation.

5. How do you feel about accountability?

Moment to **R**eflect...

Joshua 21:45 reminds us that "not a single one of all the good promises the Lord had given to the family of Israel was left unfulfilled; everything He had spoken came true."

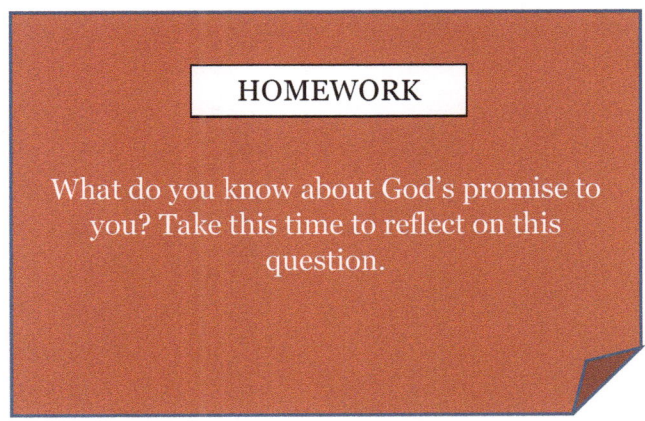

HOMEWORK

What do you know about God's promise to you? Take this time to reflect on this question.

At this party, I met his childhood friend, his college roommate, and a female cousin that had a lot of choice words for me. This one moment let me know that "Mister, Mister" had issues with his hands, fidelity problems, and an affinity for alcohol.

You would think I would have stopped answering his calls after this party. When we choose not to take the time we need to evaluate ourselves, those around us, and the patterns we have in life, we may very well end up repeating cycles of life that do not benefit us.

Bad habits can create patterns in your life that will have you on constant repeat. It took me a long time to decide to stop cycling the errors of my life. The first step was to acknowledge the habits. The second step was being held accountable for my issues.

When you take the time to pay attention to the people in your life, you will notice recurring cycles.

1. Do you see repeated cycles of drama in his personal kingdom? What are they?

2. Do you notice any broken relationships? Who do they involve?

3. Is a problem always someone else's fault?

4. Does he embrace responsibility or shrink from it?

RED ALERT:

These are warning signs. Do not miss them. They are there to protect you. Pay close attention and act accordingly.

CHAPTER 5: INTENTIONS

- ✓ **CHAOS** put out an APB (All Points Bulletin) on me.
- ✓ Somewhere along the way my heart **BETRAYED** me.
- ✓ I had to **CHOOSE**...me or my children.

Check Point!

DESCRIBE YOUR PRIORITIES	WRITE HOW MANY APPLY TO JUST YOU

It's rare that women choose themselves when they prioritize. I wrestled with myself often trying to decide to honor the woman in me. Most of the time, I chose to honor everyone else and, unfortunately, I was crushed in the process.

*Moment to **I**nspire...*

A good woman is hard to find, and
worth far more than diamonds.

~Proverbs 31:10

To get clarity about where we are going, we must write the vision. The dictionary defines vision as the ability to think about or plan the future with imagination or wisdom. There are several tools available to help you with developing your vision.

1. <u>Vision Board</u> – It's as simple as it sounds. You place pictures and/or words that display what you visualize your next goal in life should be. This is a tool that is useful for long-term or short-term goals. This will help

you become strategic about what your specific life goal truly is.

2. <u>Tree Diagram</u> – It resembles a tree with a trunk and multiple branches. It's used to depict the hierarchy of tasks and subtasks needed to complete an objective. It breaks down broad categories into finer and finer levels of detail. Developing the tree diagram helps you move your thinking, step-by-step, from generalities to specifics. It helps to answer the question, "What tasks must be done to accomplish this?"

3. <u>S.M.A.R.T. Goals</u> – Write your vision so that it is **S**pecific, **M**easurable, **A**ttainable, **R**ealistic, and **T**ime-related (**SMART**). Setting goals makes your vision more transparent. Goal setting is a powerful process for thinking about your ideal future, and for motivating yourself to turn your vision of this future into reality. By knowing precisely what you want to achieve, you know where you have to concentrate your efforts. You'll also quickly spot the distractions that can, so easily, lead you astray.

Moment to Reflect...

"I have learned that champions aren't just born; champions can be made when they embrace and commit to life-changing positive habits." — *Lewis Howes*

HOMEWORK

During your down time, go to YouTube and type "Habits of Successful People." I find this site to be very helpful in numerous ways.

You should have a clearer picture of:

- ✓ who you are
- ✓ what you want out of life
- ✓ where you're going

Now, you need to be crystal-clear that the man in your life is certain about his life's mission. A man who is not certain of his life's mission can be the most miserable person you will ever meet. He will make you miserable too, especially if you know where you want to go in life. He cannot be supportive of your achievements because he is floundering in a sea of uncertainty over his own life. He is not a healthy partner to have and to hold forever.

Below are 3 valuable lessons I've learned!

1. A man guided by a sense of destiny and purpose will not just allow life to happen around him. He would follow the vision God has given him. What vision has your man shared with you?

2. A man who has vision is not intimidated by a woman whose mission statement is clear. He will be your best ally, cheerleader and assistant because he wants you both to make it! Have you seen him cheer you on?

3. A man who prepares for your future has made his intentions clear. What preparations have you seen for your future together?

CHAPTER 6: COMPLIMENTARY

- ✓ You can't make a clear decision about what you **WANT** if you don't know what you **HAVE.**
- ✓ **TALENTS** are learned.
- ✓ **GIFTS** are something that the Heavenly Father gives His children individually.

Check Point!

WHEN YOU SHOP FOR AN OUTFIT, WHAT DO YOU CONSIDER?	WRITE A LIST OF WHAT WOULD CAUSE YOU TO LEAVE THE OUTFIT IN THE STORE

We often evaluate an outfit by the look and feel of the fabric and how it fits. Sometimes we consider the cost of the outfit by the accessories we may have to purchase. We may take the time to evaluate if we already have anything complimentary. This helps us evaluate the cost. Have you ever taken the time to consider the cost of a relationship?

Moment to *Inspire*...

But don't begin until you count the cost. For who would begin construction of a building without first calculating the cost to see if there is enough money to finish it?

~Luke 14:28

SPIRITUAL GIFTS

When you know your gifts, talents, and purpose in life, you can evaluate them against the person/things you are interested in. Gaining a better understanding of your gifts, talents, and purpose will help you during your evaluation process.

"In His grace, God has given us different gifts for doing certain things well." There are 18 different gifts listed in Romans 12:6-8, 1 Corinthians 12:8-10; 28-30, and Ephesians 4:11. People often interchange the meaning of gifts and talents, but there is a difference.

Talents are learned. A gift is something that the Heavenly Father gives His children individually. They may or may not over-lap or coincide with natural talents.

GIFTS	TALENTS
Effortless free flow drawing	Taking architecture in school
Strategic thinker	Developed organizational skills
Public speaking with ease	Toastmaster's international training
Building things without a blueprint	Building from courses taken

To develop a talent, all you have to do is find something you are interested in, learn it and practice it (and practice it) to create a talent. You can create a talent at any time in your life. A gift is something that you are, literally, born with that God has given you to use in your lifetime, in a specific way. It's that one thing you do that is effortless. You may have the same type of gift as someone else, but only you can share it in the manner God needs *you* to share.

RED ALERT:

Our gifts are blessings to help us fulfill our purpose on Earth.

Moment to Reflect...

*"The man in your life should have a healthy
love and acceptance of himself."*

- Tanya E. Hood

HOMEWORK

Read Ephesians 5:21-33: Do these passages
align with your thoughts of man and woman?
Are these traits what you expect from your
mate?

When evaluating the gifts and talents of your mate, make sure your hearts beat for mutual causes. Just like when you shop, you consider the fabric, the fit and what you already have in your closet. Decide if your relationship is a complementary addition to what you already have.

1. Do my talents and gifts complement his?

2. Do his gifts complement mine?

3. What about our temperaments?

    a. Do I see us as an effective team capable of bringing blessing to the lives of those around us?

    b. Do our futures mesh?

    c. Could we coordinate our gifts in an attractive and effective way?

This process will, probably, lead you to the "3 C's":

Clarification

Some relationships need clarifying. The two of you have been present, but you are not quite sure what to say, not quite sure what to do, and not quite sure how to deal. So, you need to clarify what it is you are expecting, and what it is that you want.

Connection

There may have been a moment or an incident that took place that drew you apart and you need to reconnect in order for your future to be strengthened.

Closure

Sometimes you have to close some things in order for you to open up some new things in your life to move forward. There are some rooms that cannot be opened unless the door behind you is closed.

The 3 C's will help you determine in which direction you are moving toward with this person. It is quite okay to have a vision of what we want from a spouse, but you should never waste time reinventing yourself or the person in your life.

Now take a moment to answer this series of questions:

1. Do you feel that you must compromise your faith to have the relationship you want?

2. Can you soar in spirit with this person, even when challenges arise?

3. Does your longing for a mate enable you to forfeit who you are in the process? Why?

CHAPTER 7: THE EXAMPLE

- ✓ I learned that my **WORTH** is defined in God.
- ✓ **TRUE LOVE** is found in the presence of God.
- ✓ My **RELATIONSHIP WITH GOD** reflects my relationship with others.

Check Point!

List a name next to each attribute:

Truly understands you: 	Willing to pay the cost to love you:
Can read your silence: 	Will stand for you at any cost:
Can bring to life various aspects of you: 	Won't allow you to compromise:
Helps you get clarity about what matters: 	Understands the depths of your soul:
Allows you to see how magnificent you are: 	Willing to die for you:

The truth of the matter is that anything worth having, costs. So, what *cost* are you putting on your worth? I would never be a valuable woman or a capable wife until I knew what it meant to truly be loved.

Moment to *I*nspire...

Before I formed you in the womb, I knew you, before you were born, I set you apart; For we are God's masterpiece. He has created us anew in Christ Jesus, so we can do the good things He planned for us long ago.

~ Jeremiah 1:5 and Ephesians 2:10

God wants to help you manifest the true being of who you are. He wants you to understand that you are worthy of being loved exactly as He intends you to be, because He made you. No one will ever pursue you like Him, love you like Him, or die for you like Him.

1. To move forward in a new relationship whole, you must discard the remnants from the past relationship. What is lingering in your soul that you have not forgiven?

2. What abuses have you allowed to penetrate your soul?

3. Dating God was a major part of healing the broken pieces in me. What would a date with God look like for you?

It's ok to wash, rinse, and repeat in the forgiving process. With each purge, you heal. It doesn't mean you weren't sincere when you forgave in the past. It simply means you are stronger now and can handle the next phase of healing needed to give your soul freedom. Be patient with yourself in your healing. Take the time to settle your past so it doesn't constantly show up in your present.

Moment to Reflect...

My time with God prepared me to be successful at being a wife when God chose my husband for me. You have to be prepared for marriage. Marriage is not easy. Marriage will show you all of your fallacies and if the man you marry is not prepared for your uniqueness, you will clash.

— Tanya E. Hood

HOMEWORK

Read Ephesians 6:10-18. We are in a spiritual battle. This is our spiritual armor. God's armor brings victory because it is far more than a protective covering. It is the very life of Jesus Christ Himself.

RED ALERT:

The Creator of the Universe decided you were worth the cost of pouring out His deity to become a man and die for your sins, just so you could get the chance to spend eternity in His embrace.

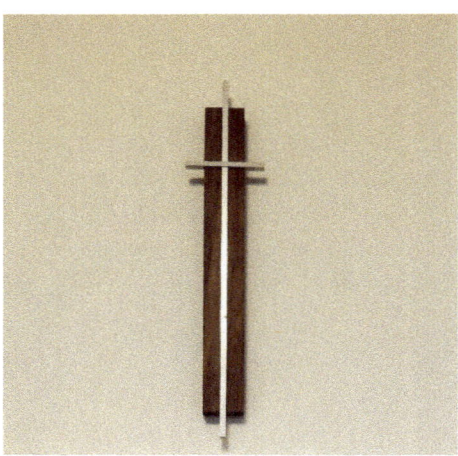

While you are still trying to figure things out, God knows who you are and loves you anyway. While you are wondering who would ever love you with all the *baggage* you carry, God knows who you are and loves you anyway.

There are so many things people say about accepting Jesus Christ that it gets confusing. God taught me that it's simple:

1. Believe in your heart.
2. Confess with your mouth that Jesus Christ is Lord and that He died and rose from the dead to save us all from sin (Acts 16:31, Romans 10:9-10).

That's it!

Salvation is God's gift to you. You have to decide to believe and trust God. If you want to experience the love, joy, and peace I have, take a moment and bow your head and pray a prayer like this one right now:

> *God, I'm sorry for my sin. I turn from it right now. I thank You for sending Jesus Christ to die on the cross for my sin. Jesus, I ask You to come into my heart and life right now; be my Lord, Savior, and friend. Help me to follow You all the days of my life. Thank You for forgiving and receiving me right now. Thank You that my sin is forgiven and that I am going to heaven. In Jesus' name I pray, Amen.*

Find a Bible-believing, Christ-centered, and Spirit-led church to help you grow and develop.

God saved you by His grace when you believed. And you can't take credit for this!

~ Ephesians 2:8

1. What is the first thing you do when you're in trouble?

2. When things get tough, how do you fight?

God has given us a spiritual inheritance that must be won in conjunction with His strength. That inheritance lies in relationships and because it lies in relationships, that is the place the enemy attacks us the most. The devil does not want you to take possession of what is rightfully yours. God has given us protection so we can fight against the enemy. There are 6 pieces of armor.

THREE PIECES YOU ARE TO WEAR AT ALL TIMES	THREE PIECES YOU PICK UP AS NEEDED
Belt of Truth	Helmet of Salvation
Breastplate of Righteousness	Shield of Faith
Shoes of Peace.	Sword of the Spirit

Once you have on your armor you need a *sealant* to keep it in place, that's called *prayer*. Prayer is simply having a conversation with God to ask heaven to intervene on your behalf.

One last thing I want you to remember:

Matthew 6:33 says, *Seek the Kingdom of God above all else, and live righteously, and he will give you everything you need.*

BONUS SECTION

NEXT LEVEL NOTES

I want to commend you for taking the time to work on being the best version of yourself. You have asked yourself the tough questions. You have worked through some difficult terrains to reach your next level. I want you to know that everything you will ever encounter, God has already prepared for. The Bible is rich with lessons, principles, and values that will help guide your life. If you take the time to study and apply the knowledge of the Word, you will be successful.

Written on the DNA of every soul is the story of the Savior. Unfortunately, not enough of us look to the right source to have the truth of that knowledge revealed. The Bible is the *roadmap*. The Holy Spirit is the *guide*. They are here to provide the individual help you need to get through this life.

Your Heavenly Father has always been present in your life. He wants you to sit at His feet to learn your worth. He wants to show you what it means to be respected. He wants to clean up the mess the world has left on your self-esteem.

I want to leave you with a prayer that has blessed my soul. I do not know the author, but the prayers is as follows:

Dear Heavenly Father,

I confess that I have not always been as careful as I should've been with my heart. From time to time, my desire for love has caused me to leave my heart in the wrong hands. I now commit my heart into Your hands for safekeeping. Please help me to stop being so impulsive with what You deem so precious. As I learn to celebrate Your love for me, let me learn from Your example what a bridegroom should really be like. Help me to never settle for less than what You desire for me. As I embrace You as the Lover of my soul, keep my affections in the haven of Your Own heart. As I rest in Your love, make me more discriminating of those who approach me. I ask that You take over this area of my life. Keep me from those You know would hurt my heart. I invite You to set a hedge around me and keep me from all who would draw me into unfruitful relationships until the day You present me to the mate that You have selected for me. Grant me the discernment to recognize him as he recognizes me. Cleanse me from the temptation to typecast the men I meet according to what I see. Help me to trust in Your knowledge and lean not on my own understanding. I know that You know what is best for me; therefore, I yield to Your choice. In Jesus' Name, Amen.

ABOUT THE AUTHOR

Tanya E. Hood is a wife, mother, and business owner. And as early as 8 years old, this Washington, D.C. native dreamed of giving back to her community, and bettering the lives of others. That's why it comes as no surprise that she is the author of ***Red Alert! Is He The One? Pocket Guide To Finding The Love Of Your Life***.

Her pocket guide was birthed from hard lessons in love that, now, enable readers to achieve more love, more happiness, & more fulfilling relationships. And the proof that these lessons work, can be found in her happy marriage to Eric B. Hood, author of *It's All About ME: Motivation and Encouragement*, and in her relationship with their 3 children (Erica M. Hood, Derrick M Butler II, and Justice D.C. Butler).

Tanya's list of accolades and accomplishments are numerous. Combining her Pre-Engineering studies from Dunbar SHS, her Electrical Engineering degree from Howard University, and her strong faith in God, she is on a mission to inspire, motivate, and create lasting change in her community. She uses a full range of strategies and skills to provide life-changing solutions to her readers and clients. She is Chief Executive Officer of Source Trinity Homes, LLC., Vice President of the Nuclear Regulatory Commission B.I.G. Chapter, and the 1st Place Winner of Toastmaster's 2018 Table Topics Contest (Area 65, District 36).

Confident, committed, and compassionate, Tanya remains an active member of First Baptist Church of Highland Park, in Landover, MD, and uses her free time to volunteer to help men, women, and children in her community.

Tanya E. Hood

To purchase Red Alert! Is He the One?
(Pocket Guide) ©2014, 2017
ISBN 10 - 0996995382
ISBN 13 - 978-0-9969953-8-2
TanyaEHood.com
http://bit.ly/redalertpocketguide

Also available on Kindle

FOLLOW ME

https://www.facebook.com/RedAlertIsHeTheOne/

https://www.instagram.com/redalertishetheone/

https://twitter.com/TanyaEHood

https://www.youtube.com/channel/UCB8uBV_q1-kI2kfNSAdanug?view_as=subscriber

https://www.pinterest.com/tanyaehood/

https://www.linkedin.com/in/tanya-hood-6064b073/

CPSIA information can be obtained
at www.ICGtesting.com
Printed in the USA
BVHW021534220719
554071BV00019B/583/P